FAMINE, HUNGER AND STARVATION IN AFRICA:
Challenge To African and World Leaders

by

Dr. John Karefah Marah

Bloomington, IN  Milton Keynes, UK

authorHOUSE™

AuthorHouse™
1663 Liberty Drive, Suite 200
Bloomington, IN 47403
www.authorhouse.com
Phone: 1-800-839-8640

AuthorHouse™ UK Ltd.
500 Avebury Boulevard
Central Milton Keynes, MK9 2BE
www.authorhouse.co.uk
Phone: 08001974150

First published by AuthorHouse 5/5/2006

ISBN: 1-4259-2828-5 (sc)

Printed in the United States of America
Bloomington, Indiana

This book is printed on acid-free paper.

Series Editor: Kofi Quaye
Heritage/Mysteek Contemporary Global Perspectives

Table of Contents

Chapter One

Africa's Natural Resources

The natural resources of Africa are numerous, despite the current famine resulting in the starvation of millions of Africans throughout the continent. Africa's natural resources can be utilized effectively to raise the standard of living of Africans in Africa and elsewhere. What is needed in Africa now and in the future is to aggressively exploit the natural and human resources in an organized fashion so that those areas of the continent that are lacking in some resources can be reached quickly with resources from other parts of the continent that have certain resources in abundance.

The continent of Africa is second only to Asia and three-to-four times as large as the United States. Sudan, the largest country in Africa, is about a fourth the size of the United States. With a total area of 11,684,000 square miles and an estimated population of 480 people per square mile,[1] the African continent is one of the least populated areas of the world. The most densely populated country in Africa, Burundi, has six people per square mile.[2] The Nile, the longest river on earth, is in Africa, and flows north from Lake Victoria for more than four thousand miles to the Mediterranean Sea.[3] Lake Victoria, the largest lake on the continent, covers more than 26,000 square miles, approximately 250 miles long, 150 miles wide, and is bordered by Kenya, Uganda and Rwanda.[4] Africa has other natural wonders such as deep valleys, large waterfalls, deep fresh water lakes and the largest desert in the world, covering parts of Sudan, Egypt, Libya, Chad, Mali, Mauritania, Algeria and Morocco.[5] Even though much of the land in these countries is in desert or near desert condition, they have natural resources that could be exploited for consumer goods and to raise the general standard of living of the people. Mauritania has large deposits of iron ore, copper and gypsum, which are still unexploited. Algeria has petroleum as its primary resource, as well as large deposits of gold, platinum and diamonds. The only desert countries so far known to be poor in natural resources are Mali and Chad, even though they produce cotton, and there is some evidence that points to the existence of oil, uranium and bauxite, especially in Chad.

For the 'non-desert' countries, Guinea has large deposits of bauxite, iron ore, manganese and copper, and its climate is conducive to the growing of various types of crops and livestock. Zambia, in Southeastern Africa, is known for its large deposits of copper: the Zambezi River and its tributaries supply abundant water in addition to the many lakes within the country. "In Gabon in northwest Central Africa, there is a very large deposit of nearly a billion tons of proven

2

reserve of rich iron ore."[6] The Central African Republic is also known for its vast areas of timber, and has deposits of uranium and diamonds. "South Africa today is the predominant world producer of gold, having an output of some 23 million ounces, almost three times larger than that of the second producer, the Soviet Union."[7]

Other African countries are naturally endowed. "Zaire and Zambia," for instance, "are the world's leading producers of cobalt, an important hardener and strengthener of steel, used, for example, in jet engines. The United States imports about 95 percent of the cobalt it uses, three quarters coming from Zaire."[8] Angola, Swaziland, Liberia, and other African countries export iron ore to the west, principally to the United States.

In addition to iron ore, diamonds, bauxite, chromite and other non-fuel natural resources, many African countries have oil deposits. The significant producers of oil in Africa are Nigeria, Libya, Gabon, Angola, the Congo Republic, Cameroon, and Zaire. "Oil has also been discovered in West Africa off the coasts of Ghana, the Ivory Coast, Liberia, and Senegal."[9] These oil fields have not been fully exploited, and when industrialized they could revolutionize Africa's economy.

The continent of Africa has great hydroelectric power potential, which, if properly and strategically utilized, could also revolutionize Africa's economy and lifestyle. "The greatest hydroelectric potential

3

in Africa is Zaire (132 million kw.), Madagascar (64 million kw.), Cameroon (23 million kw.), Tanzania (21 million kw.), Gabon (18 million kw.), and Sudan (16 million kw.). Kenya, Uganda, Upper Volta, the Central African Republic, and Niger also have considerable potential."[10] It is important to note that the African countries endowed with hydroelectric potential are distributed throughout the continent, including the island of Madagascar. These resources, when properly coordinated, should be able to supply those areas not so endowed. Furthermore, "hydropower can eliminate the need to expensively import oil for the production of electricity."[11] Zambia, Zimbabwe, Zaire, and Ghana already are using this source of power minimally. In addition to mining and hydroelectric potential in the continent of Africa, all of which are currently underutilized, agriculture is the most predominant occupation of the people of Africa. "It also produces between 40 and 60 per cent of the gross national product in all countries, except Botswana, Gabon, and Zambia, where mining is particularly important."[12] Most Africans continue to engage in subsistence farming in rural areas; others are cattle rearers, such as the Fulani in West Africa, and the Masai in Kenya, East Africa. In the southern portion of the continent, there is considerable migrant labor, but women and the elderly still tend to the soil. Despite the Sahara, heavy tropical rains, especially in Central Africa, that tend to deplete the soil of some valuable ingredients for the productive growing of crops, Africa's agricultural potential cannot be underestimated. And since the majority of Africans are farmers and continue to derive their sustenance from the soil, Africa's agricultural potential must be urgently studied so as to increase production.

That Africa's natural resources are numerous and should be progressively exploited cannot be questioned, but with the current large scale starvation in Africa, one cannot help but be curious as to why, with all these natural and human resources, there is still large scale starvation in Africa. Ethiopia, Sudan, Somalia, Niger and other African countries are losing many lives because of the lack of food and water. Although many African countries such as Malawi, Ivory Coast, Cameroon and Gabon are able to feed themselves, a large number of Africans who are not actually starving suffer from hunger and malnutrition, poor housing and illiteracy.

What are some of the salient factors that have contributed to starvation in Africa? Why are the human and the natural resources of Africa not being used to increase agricultural and industrial production? Is the aid Africa is receiving from abroad a solution? How do people of African descent in the West feel about the starvation in Africa? Has the food aid program from the West and East become a political rather than a humanitarian game? How do Africans, with just a few years of independence, feel about the deterioration of their economies? These are some of the questions that those who have been bombarded with news of the continuing starvation in Africa have been discreetly or publicly asking. In the following chapters we attempt to deal with some of these questions. But first, which are the afflicted countries, and to what extent is starvation rampant in Africa?

Chapter Two

The Afflicted Countries

European and American media, especially television, tend to focus on Ethiopia and Somalia as though they are the only African countries experiencing famine. Regrettably, Somalia could easily be the one country experiencing the worst starvation: more than a million children and adult peasants have lost their lives within the last few years.

The purpose of this chapter is to try to classify African countries into three major categories: (1) the severely affected countries; (2) the moderately affected countries; and (3) those African countries that are, at the present, able to feed themselves. It must be noted, however, that most African countries suffer from some form of malnutrition, hunger, disease, and inadequate housing, especially among the illiterates and peasants who mostly face abnormal food shortages. Furthermore, most African countries have had declines in their agricultural production after political independence.

Nonetheless, the following African countries can be categorized as the severely afflicted nations in East Africa:

Djibouti	Rwanda
Tanzania	Sudan
Ethiopia	Somalia

These six East African countries have been hardest hit by drought and the subsequent drop in agricultural production, thus drastically increasing the need to import food from the West. The need for food imports in these countries has progressively increased, especially in the form of cereals and wheat, but since their agricultural production has declined, food aid has been their major source of subsistence.

In Southern Sudan, the decline in agricultural production has been compounded by the influx of "more than 100,000 refugees from the drought-stricken north.... The shortages are further aggravated by the presence of at least 200,000 Ethiopian refugees in the east – reportedly arriving at a daily rate of 2,500 – and the Chadian refugees in the west."[1] Somalia has, since the late 1970's, suffered from lack of rainfall which has affected the growing of bananas and the herding of camels, sheep, goats and cattle on which the peasants depend for subsistence. "The crippling weather aside, Ethiopia and Somalia are still nursing the wounds of the 1977/78 Ogaden war, which displaced large populations and fueled the continuing civil strife, further complicating food production and distribution in both nations."[2] In addition, Sudan and Somalia have fought civil wars and both countries have had poor relations with Ethiopia. In parts of both

Kenya and Tanzania, the lack of rainfall has left some farmlands sun-scorched and impotent for agricultural production. Thus, in Eastern Africa drought, civil wars and refugees have essentially contributed to the shortage of food.

Other African countries that have severely experienced starvation are:

Chad	Mali
Mauritania	Niger
Senegal	Burkina Faso [formerly Upper Volta]
Cape Verde	Zambia
Botswana	Lesotho
Angola	Zimbabwe
Mozambique	

Here again, drought, in addition to other factors, have deteriorated agricultural production. "At least 100,000 persons in Mozambique were believed to have died from starvation in 1984 and despite recent improvements, life for many remains grim."[3] Both Botswana and Angola have experienced inadequate rainfall. Aside from the drought in Northern Angola, UNITA, supported by South Africa, continued its guerilla activities in the South and Central regions where crop production seemed to be effective and the climate conducive.

In Western Africa, the Sahelian countries such as Mali, Mauritania, Niger, Burkina Faso, etc. have all experienced famine because of the lack of rainfall. Guinea has had crop failures in the north due to drought and with the expected return "...of hundreds of thousands of Guineans who had been living in exile in neighboring countries,"[4] food shortages are expected to be acute. Already "faced with a 11% decline in per capita production since 1969-71 period, Guinea has been relying on imports to cover its food deficit as much as 40,000 tons of cereals in 1982."[5]

The seven Sahelian West African countries, the six East African countries, and six countries in Southern Africa experienced acute starvation and have been in desperate need for food aid. In all these acute cases, the adult population and their children are the victims of starvation.

There are other African countries that have been moderately affected by drought, increased urbanization, and decreased agricultural production. Though there is no large scale starvation in these countries, there is malnutrition and hunger, especially among the rural population. The five North African countries of Egypt, Morocco, Algeria, Tunisia and Libya fall into this category; "...all five states have managed to feed their people with the help of considerable foreign aid (especially in Egypt, Morocco and Tunisia) and revenues from the development of petrochemical resources (Libya, Algeria)."[6] These countries have not been seriously affected by the drought or desertification "...for these Mediterranean countries have been for long accustomed to cultivating the narrow strip of arable land sandwiched between the sea and the Sahara, plus the Nile Valley and a few stable oases."[7]

In West Africa, countries such as Sierra Leone, Liberia and Nigeria are moderately affected. Liberia and Sierra Leone are affected because they are "...plagued by low yields of rice."[8] Nigeria has experienced drought in the North and decreased agricultural production to some extent. "Nigerian agriculture also suffers from a labor shortage, as many young people move to urban areas."[9] The five North African countries, Nigeria, Sierra Leone and Liberia are affected more by large scale rural-urban migration that reduces rural agricultural production and puts heavy strains on urban facilities. Here, consumer goods become expensive, shortage of export crops reduces the nations' capacity for surplus to import basic goods and results in a general decline in the standard of living. In the absence of large scale industrialization, there is considerable unemployment of the masses who are forced to live in city slums and experience malnutrition and other diseases; the Liberian civil war added to the problem in the region.

To a certain extent, several African countries have been able to feed their populations: Uganda, Swaziland, Malawi, Ivory Coast, Togo, Gabon, Cameroon, Congo, Zaire, Benin, and the Union of South Africa have been able to steadily increase their food production. "...partly due to the oil reserves in Cameroon, Congo and Gabon, the region has tended to out-perform the rest of the continent economically."[10] Furthermore, those African countries that have been able to feed their populace tend to, though not exclusively, "...lie on or near the equator, where climates are characterized by high humidities, high temperatures and high rainfalls, as in equatorial Guinea, Gabon, Sao Tome and Principe and parts of Zaire. The main food crops are cassava – a crop high in carbohydrates that is drought resistant and gives high yields even in less fertile soil – and other roots and tubers."[11] In addition, natural conditions favoring food production and some governmental policies on agriculture have also added to improved agricultural production in these last set of African countries.

Africa, as a continent, has generally experienced declining food production, abandonment of rural areas, political corruption, mismanagement of national funds, high birthrate and a "...very high level of dependence upon agricultural exports for foreign exchange earnings."[12] While Africa is being 'advised' to specialize in agriculture, Western countries continue to improve in technology.

While it is crucial for Africa to increase food production, it is also imperative that African countries actively initiate and pursue policies designed to mechanize its process of farming. However, to 'fully' grasp and understand starvation in Africa, various factors must be understood. The impact of the lack of technological sophistication has been low food production and low standard of living for the African masses, malnutrition and others associated with underdevelopment.

Chapter Three

Why Starvation in Africa

The continued large scale starvation in Africa is caused by a number of factors, most of which are political, economical, social, cultural, traditional, technical, international, as well as national. Millions of Africans have and are still starving because of the lack of food, water and shelter. The victims of starvation are children, women and men in Africa's rural areas where the majority of African people reside and tend to their daily wants and needs. In addition to the starving population in rural areas, poor urban settlers, mostly illiterate, and the partially educated and school drop-outs, face extreme malnutrition.

The purpose of this chapter is to attempt to account for some of the salient factors associated with the continued large scale starvation in Africa. The British and American media have focused considerable attention on the starvation in Somalia, Ethiopia, Sudan, and the Sahelian countries and have generally emphasized civil wars, weather conditions and problems of refugees migrating from one African country into another. Nonetheless, starvation in Africa is also a manifestation of Africa's extreme underdevelopment, a view shared by many experts all over the world.

Production vs. Distribution: "To many, the problem is insufficient production…. The other main argument holds that the food problem is one of the distribution of foodstuffs which are of themselves adequate in supply but unevenly available."[1] Support for the credibility of this dual position would not be hard to illustrate; the educated urbanite in Africa is conspicuously better fed, housed and enjoys modern facilities in abundance, and to some extent flamboyantly. On the other hand, shanty houses of cardboard, crowded rooms and the absence of modern facilities characterize the existence of many of the poor urbanites. This is true all over Africa; the few live in abundant luxury, the majority in abject poverty. It is generally true that Africa's natural resources are nowhere nearly equally distributed. That the African peasant has produced less in view of the rise in population is true to a great extent, but the educated African has produced far less in post-colonial Africa; he has consumed more than he has produced.

With respect to Africa and the Western world in terms of production and distribution, the developed countries in the West have been able to produce surplus food for internal consumption, as well as for exportation while Africa continues to be, literally, an international beggar of food. Within the developed countries, however, there is the poor, working-and-ill- housed. Indeed, Africa's "…poverty is

a handicap and a threat, both to them and the prosperous areas."[2]
This becomes clearer when we cross national boundaries and realize
that victims of starvation, malnutrition and bad housing are usually
workers and peasants in all societies. "The problems of bringing
the fruits of the world's abundant productivity to those who most
need them are political and administrative, rather than economic
or scientific..."[3] That is, to a certain extent at least. In Africa, the
problems of production and distribution seem to be more urgent than
in the developed countries and other developed regions of the world.
Even within Africa, countries such as Ivory Coast, Libya, Cameroon,
etc., because of governmental policies and availability of technical
know-how, have been able to feed their populations better than most
other African countries.

Farming Methods in Africa: Farming methods in Africa are
largely ineffective, resulting in their failure to feed the growing
population in urban areas where the majority are not agriculturists
or producers of some kind, but mainly consumers of imported goods
from the developed countries.

> The simplest form of agriculture...still the general practice in
> most of Africa...where land is comparatively abundant, is to cut
> down and burn a patch of forest or scrub, thereby both fertilizing
> the ground and clearing it of weeds, though leaving it somewhat
> deficient in organic matter and nitrogen, and then to plant seeds
> in the ashes. In the course of years of growth, the deep roots of
> trees have brought up from the subsoil and leave in the ashes
> comparatively abundant supplies of the mineral elements.

However, the soil fertility obtained by this method soon falls off. The cultivation is then abandoned, and a fresh patch of scrub or forest cleared.[4]

This shifting cultivation progressively destroys forests and in the long run accelerates desertification. The Fulani in West Africa, the Masai in Kenya and the Nomads of Somalia are known to be cattle rearers and often burn extensive areas of grassland for their cattle to feed on tender and young grass. Until they are educated as to their interdependence on nature, they will continue to use such methods to their peril and the land as well. As they depend on their cattle, and as their cattle must feed on grass, their contribution to desertification over a long period of time cannot be underestimated, as it has already become apparent.

Effects of Erosion: Africa is largely a tropical continent, and even though this doesn't give rise to unproductive soil conditions, it does mean that heavy tropical rains do deplete the soil of some of its nutrients. During the two seasons of heavy rainfalls and hot sunshine in the rainy and dry periods, there is much soil erosion and evaporation of water from the earth and plants. Furthermore, when African peasant farmers plant their crops on hills with sharp slopes, the top soil is eroded, leaving the land with minimal nutrients for effective food production.

"Erosion at first appears in the form of some of the topsoil being removed and carried away as silt in the streams. If extensive, erosion leads to a loss of soil fertility. In its worst form gullies appear in the soil, gradually increasing in size, until it becomes impossible to cultivate the land."[5]

The problem is compounded with the lack of modernized agricultural machinery in the hands of most African peasants, resulting in large tracts of lands losing their capacity to be fertile and productive.

Desertification: The African continent has the largest desert on earth – the Sahara – covering Sudan, Egypt, Libya, Chad, Niger, Mali, Mauritania, Algeria and Morocco; in effect, an extensive area of the African continent. It is also the case that the Sahara desert is increasing and expanding southwards, and without effective and massive reforestation, the Sahara would in the long run expand into more African countries. At present, the Sahara claims up to three million square miles. [6]

Overpopulation: "Africa is not overpopulated and is not threatened with overpopulation." The problem in Africa currently is "how many people can an area (such as Nairobi or Lagos) accommodate adequately and still progress economically and socially."[7] Similarly, how many people can the Sahelian region accommodate and still progress economically, socially and culturally?

The rural-urban migration in Africa has been extensively cited by geographers, urban planners and others as contributing to poor housing and a burden to Africa's urban facilities. The youth concentration in urban areas has deprived rural areas of the able labor force to at least maintain subsistence-existence of the African peasants; thus, the underpopulation of arable rural areas has contributed to the decline in food production. "...economic backwardness as a whole is the chief and crucial factor behind the aggravation of the food problem,"[8] not overpopulation per se, at least in the case of continental Africa.

Transportation Problems: The lack of well developed road systems in Africa deters the fast movement of goods and services, even the delay of food aid to those areas that need it most. And "where you have no roads, and are too poor even to keep draft animals, head porterage is the only possible form of transport; and travelers are indeed amazed at the skill with which Africans and Asians can balance heavy loads on the tops of their heads."[9] But such loads can hardly feed a village or an extended family for a long period of time.

Health: The health of African people on the continent is poor: Kwashiorkor, tuberculosis, AIDS, blindness, leprosy, malaria, smallpox, measles and bilharzia and others take their toll on the work capacity of a large segment of the African populace. "By the time an African child reaches adulthood there is a good chance that he will be feebled by one of the many parasitic diseases rampant on the continent."[10] The African child's productive capacity will be drastically reduced as one of these common diseases goes on, without treatment, for an extended period of time.

The continuing large scale starvation in Africa is certainly bound to retard the physical and mental capacity of those who would survive. Thus, a good number of African 'youth' would remain peripheral to the production of new ideas and material goods for generations to come.

"To combat sickness in Africa, one of the first necessities is the creation of new attitudes towards health."[11] And a similar statement with respect to African people's attitudes towards work must be made. As African countries embark on industrialization or scientific agriculture, as they must, they must create positive attitudes towards work, time, productivity and safety. This becomes extremely important in view of the fact that "...rapid urban growth places a strain on existing health facilities and creates a demand for health care greater than a city's capacity to construct and staff new health centers."[12] The underprivileged sections of African cities consequently become disease infested, and sick people are economically unproductive and must be treated at the family and the nation's expense, and thus, an additional strain on the meager resources.

<u>Subsistence: Tradition in Africa</u>: Africa's low agricultural production is due to several factors, one of which is cultural tradition. Generally, "...the idea of surplus production is alien to many African farmers, for most Africans have led a subsistence existence for centuries."[13] And in their illiteracy, this attitude of subsistence remains dominant and difficult to eradicate.

> In pre-colonial Africa the dominant means of production reflected the needs of a family and the widespread availability of land, and thus was characterized by low productivity per acre, and per person. Little pressure existed to increase this level of output for reasons which included problems of storage within a tropical environment and problems of transportation from potential source regions to recipient areas. Even in areas with very centralized political systems, the ruling elite was more likely to exploit long distance trade or the labor of neighboring groups than to demand production increases among indigenous farmers.[14]

<u>The Colonial Legacy</u>: In the strictest terms, all African countries were once colonies. Ethiopia was briefly colonized by Italians in 1936, Liberia by Americo-Liberians and their missionary benefactors. "... the legacy of colonialism remains a big problem for African farmers today."[15] The colonialists promoted the growing of cash crops and alienated large tracts of fertile lands where these cash crops could be grown "and dismantled patterns of communal ownership"[16] of land. The Kenyan European settlers' rapacity over Kenyan Highlands, the large tracts of rubber and cocoa plantations in Ivory Coast and Ghana

respectively, peanuts and palm trees in Gambia and Sierra Leone respectively are but a few examples.

> ...the new crops required vastly different nutrients and brought intensive cultivation to soils for which such methods were unsuitable. This ultimately led to reliance on inputs – fertilizers, herbicides, pesticides – which had to be imported. Transport and marketing systems were geared to the export crop. And, when men were drawn into cash-cropping by the colonial authorities, women frequently lost the labor of husbands and sons in the family fields. These disruptions had severe effects on African societies and their economic patterns. But in the view of some experts, the ecological result – damage to soils – has equally dire implications for the long term.[17]

In African countries where mining was heavily undertaken by colonial authorities, young men were recruited away from the farms, greatly reducing rural agricultural productive capacities. The colonial authorities provided mining towns, literally shanty towns, where wage earning was the dominant economic activity. In African countries where the growing of cotton, tobacco and peanuts was done on large plantations, many Africans became plantation hands so they could earn money to purchase imported goods and pay taxes to the colonial government. Again, the youth were drawn away from their family farms and the traditional African practice of having all family members have an input into the family's economic unit was greatly undermined. Furthermore, large plantations, such as the growing of cotton in Mali, "...necessitated clearing large areas of the original cover of forest and brush."[18] And large plantations of crops such as cotton and tobacco tended "...to absorb unusually large quantities of nutrients from the topsoil, and the cumulative result has been to launch an apparently irreversible circle of deterioration and to convert large areas of Africa...to desert or semi-desert in a century's time."[19]

Neo-colonialism: African governments did not radically deviate from the colonial patterns of agricultural development; as African nationalists took over the organs of governments in the 1960s, they continued to produce single cash crops as demanded by the ex-colonial powers and to satisfy their needs. The new governments found that they needed "cash to promote diversification,...for social services and cash for debt-servicing."[20] The new African leaders found that they couldn't easily abandon the already entrenched practice of producing export crops and continued "...to spend more money on developing this sector."[20] This continued emphasis on growing exportable crops undermined the growing of, for instance, rice which had to be imported by countries like Sierra Leone that once was an exporter of this staple food.

Political Corruption: For a good number of African nationalists in the 1960s and the present, African political independence meant self-aggrandizement, use of government funds for personal purposes and for the upliftment of their families, districts and tribal members. While Nkrumah was advocating socialism or state capitalism in

Ghana in the 1960s, his ministers and other bureaucrats were busy enriching themselves.[22] Mobutu's exploitation of Zaire's wealth in natural resources is an epitome of political corruption in Africa. Mobutu is reported as selling Zairean copper and diamonds and diverting the money for his personal use. It is alleged that members of his family enriched themselves in a similar fashion. In addition to the sale of diamonds, gold, cobalt, copper, "the Mobutu clan (was) also deeply involved in the smuggling of...tea; in particular Mobutu's late wife, Marie Antoinette, who died in 1977, was involved in the management of the (tea) plantations."[23]

Stanley Shapashina Oloitiptip, a Masai, Minister of Home Affairs, Local Government, and Culture and Social Services, in the Kenyan government, was exposed for using government money for his own aggrandizement. For Oloitiptip, "Uhuru (was) a very sweet commodity because it...enabled me to own several sleek cars, a 12-room house, 12 wives and 67 children."[24]

Several other African governments and individual leaders could be shown to have been less concerned about the masses of rural Africans, and their programs have been directly concentrated on the improvement of urban areas and particular villages where the dignitaries come from; a political corruption of this nature and others have led to coups and counter-coups especially in black Africa, which have often removed legitimate and progressive African governments and leaders. Corruption in political leadership is easily and directly transferred to the bureaucrats and the populace at large in the form of smuggling and a thriving black market.

History of Exploitation: For more than 400 years the history of exploitation of man by man in Africa has been chronicled. When the Europeans arrived at the Cape of Good Hope in 1652, they defeated the cattle-raising Khoikhoi, and today, it is the South African whites who mostly auction cattle, not the Khoikhois. The land of the Xhosas was expropriated and the same was done to the lands of the Zulu in Natal. Africans were brought as slaves from other parts of Africa to work for the European settlers. This was abolished in 1833, but Indians were brought in to provide further cheap labor. The land question in South Africa has not been rectified between blacks and whites, as the case in Zimbabwe has now clearly demonstrated.

In Eastern Africa, Kenya, with its cool climate and fertile highlands reminiscent of the British countryside, was the choice spot for European settlers in the early 1900s. The Kenya Highlands was so attractive to the Europeans that extensive immigration was encouraged by British authorities between 1904 and the 1950s; the Kikuyus and other African peoples were alienated from their lands and forced to settle in areas designated by the European settlers. Kipande, or pass laws similar to those of South Africa, were promulgated; a man such as Lord Delamere was able to amass large tracts of land,

25

obtain cheap labor and enrich himself to an extent he could possibly not have attained in his native land, England. Today, it is not the European settlers or the Western-educated Africans who are starving in northern Kenya or Somalia, but the native Africans.

King Leopold's Congo was extremely exploited and the native Africans were forced to labor for their colonial masters and kept in a position of servitude all through colonial times. The Africans were forced to plant crops, trees and other commodities demanded by the colonial powers (see Adam Hochschild's <u>King Leopold's Ghost,</u> Houghton Mifflin, 1999).

In Portuguese Africa, a similar level of exploitation took place, and "since the colonies were thought to be provinces of Portugal, it was unthinkable that they should be set free."[25] Not surprisingly, therefore, the Portuguese colonies of Guinea-Bissau, Angola, and Mozambique became the last to attain political independence in Africa.

The economic exploitation of Africa and African peoples became pronounced as Europeans arrived on the continent. Before the Europeans, the Arabs had taken large numbers of African slaves into Egypt, Iran and Iraq.[26] During European contact with Africa, slavery became a predominant preoccupation and it was mostly the young, and able-bodied men and women who became victims in that momentous, but infamous episode in history. But it was not only productive human beings who were taken out of Africa; Europeans were in search of profit, and therefore began to trade with Africans in other goods as well.

In his *The History of the Upper Guinea Coast, 1545-1800*, Walter Rodney provides data to illustrate that Europe had been extracting economic surplus from Africa since the 1500s; and this relationship has existed to the present time.[27] A Captain Thomas Phillips bought an iron bar in London for 3 shillings and 6 pence and sold it on the West African coast for 7 shillings.[28] An iron bar bought in Lisbon for 6 shillings and 3 pence was sold to Africans on the West Coast for 11 shillings and 3 pence, and this same item was sold for 22 shillings and 6 pence in the hinterlands.[29] Certainly, the African chiefs and astute middlemen profited from this trade, but so also are the African leaders and their bureaucratic bourgeoisies today from the sale of Africa's raw materials. As it was then, so is it today that Africans display

> a weakness and indeed an obsession with European commodities, and, given this fatal flaw, the tragedy unfolded inexorably...yet those European consumer goods contributed nothing to the development of African production. Only the rulers benefited narrowly, by receiving the best cloth, drinking the most alcohol, and preserving the widest collection of durable items for prestige purposes.[30]

Thus, Oloitiptip's declaration that Uhuru brought him "...several sleek cars, a 12-room house, 12 wives and 67 children"[31] does not now seem out of the historical context in terms of the collaboration of the African ruling classes with their European allies in the exploitation of the African masses and Africa's natural resources; the historical and the current records of political corruption attest to that in several African nations.

Africa in the Context of the World Economy: Economic development theorists such as Samir Amin, Babu, Kwame Nrumah and Walter Rodney have posited additional reasons to explain Africa's economic underdevelopment. The current large scale starvation in Africa is the epitome of underdevelopment, and the economic development theorists assert that Africa, as is the case with most developing countries in Asia and Latin America, is at the periphery in the context of the world economy, while Western Europe and North America form the core. The core countries have been able to produce abundant food and gain high-level technical know-how for internal consumption as well as for exportation, in part, because of their continued exploitation of the raw materials from the Third World countries, a relationship established during colonialism. And as Walter Rodney has established in his *How Europe Underdeveloped Africa*,[32] this relationship of the economic exploitation of Africa has persisted. European nations would sell their products, mostly consumer-luxury goods, to balkanized African countries at exorbitant, metropolitan prices and buy African agricultural products cheaply. This relationship

28

has progressively left African countries without surplus to deal with the problems of housing, illiteracy, medicine and others, and are dependent on the demands of a world market controlled by Africa's ex-colonizers. Nationalists who came to power in the 1960s, as their records have shown, "...aimed to get rid of the colonial powers' direct rule but at the same time expressed their desire to continue economic links with the same colonial powers."[33] This continued relationship with their ex-colonizers has not resulted in the economic development of Africa, and "...because of our dependency," writes Professor Babu, "we are unable to change the course of our development even when it is clear that the path we are on is leading us nowhere."[34]

Only One Commodity to Sell: One of the strategies that has impeded the growth of the economies of most African countries has been Africa's continued dependence on the sale of only raw materials, mainly agricultural products such as coffee, palm products, cotton, cocoa, tobacco, peanuts, wheat, rubber, rice, sugar, pyrethrum, palm kernels, cinnamon and coconut products, and natural resources such as diamonds, gold, iron ore, chrome, and other raw industrial materials which they export, while they continue to import consumer goods, machinery and transport equipment, food, beverages, chemicals, etc. Much of the industry in Africa is concerned with the production of luxury items and remains as low as two percent in countries like Benin.[35] The low level of industrial development in Africa then becomes one of the crucial factors associated with underdevelopment and starvation in Africa.

False Ideologies and Charlatan Experts: Africa is the Tower of Babel for foreign ideologies, more so than any other continent in the world. On the African continent, there are proclaimed Marxists, Scientific Socialists, African Socialists, Nkrumaltists, Humanists, Pan-Africanists, Authenticists, and a myriad of nameless others, yet none that has proved itself viable and objective enough to greatly improve the living conditions of the masses of the African peoples. Okot P'Bitek criticized African Socialist Tanzania as a "…government of the people by the educated for the educated."[36] Mobutu's authenticity obviously meant his own personal enrichment. Nigeria's adoption of the American federal form of government has been affected by large scale bureaucratic corruption, Ethiopia's claim of Marxism did not revolutionize the feudal land system, Nkrumah's Pan-Africanism under socialism was not endorsed by the majority of the African leadership. One can cite many more regimes in Africa that have embarked on an ideology such as non-alignment, which has not solved their problems.

When African countries attained political independence in the 1960s and the early 1970s, they continued to rely on Western or Eastern experts to advise them on how best to develop their countries and the continent of Africa. The foreign experts were often advocates of their own (home) systems of thought and paradigms. They were often not committed to genuine African development and saw African problems through the Western or Eastern perspective. Thus, most of their recommendations for African development have ended in failure. They may have received their Ph.Ds in Anthropology or African Economics, but their recommendations have not had an iota of positive effect on African development.

The Elimination of Radical African Leaders: African political and intellectual leaders who have stood for the total upliftment of the African masses have been systematically opposed or eliminated by the enemies of African peoples in collaboration with their African bureaucratic bourgeois, military and police agents. The names of such positive leaders are too numerous to be mentioned, but a few outstanding leaders can be cited: Patrice Lumumba, J.M. Karuiki, Malcolm X, Walter Rodney, Amilcar Cabral, Steve Biko, Dedan Kimathi, Michael Manley, Kwame Nkrumah, Oginga Odinga, Mandela, etc. And as their records have shown since the 1960s, the majority of African leaders have not greatly contributed to African development, and have sometimes contributed to the deterioration of African economies despite, for most of them, their more than twenty years as leaders of government, or as fathers of their African nations.

Education: Irrespective of the seemingly massive efforts of African leaders of the 'sixties and the seventies' to mass-educate Africa,

> ...in education, generally, Africa is the most backward region of the world. Its universities, unit by unit, are the smallest in number of any other major world region, and continue to have the lowest ratio of students enrolled as a percentage of the twenty-to-twenty-four-year age group, Asia having four times the number of university students per capita, and Latin America, five.[37]

If one were to compare Africa to America in terms of the number of students and educational institutions, Africa would indeed be clearly seen to have accomplished little.[38]

Perhaps Africa's backwardness in education can best be illustrated by the level of illiteracy (Table 1).[39] Even though some African countries, such as Tanzania, Botswana, Lesotho, etc. have attempted to increase literacy of both males and females, most African countries can be seen to have largely illiterate societies, especially the female population. Until illiteracy is eliminated in Africa, African peoples will continue to be politically, technically, and economically backward. The majority of Africans will continue to be peripheral to the political process, the choosing of political leadership, and thus the existence of corrupt leaders such as the late Mobutu of Zaire[40] and even the continued existence of "apartheid in disguise" in Post Apartheid South Africa and a discriminated Black

America. The following concerning illiteracy could illuminate the predicament of the mass of African people, to a certain extent:

TABLE 1

AFRICAN LITERACY RATES, 1985

COUNTRY	% OF MALES	% OF FEMALES	OFFICIAL LANGUAGE
Angola	36	19	Portuguese
Benin	43	17	French
Botswana	37	44	Setswana/English
Burundi	39	16	Kirundi/French
Cameroon	55	25	French
Cape Verde	54	34	Portuguese
Central African Republic	48	20	French
Chad	12	1	French
Comoros	66	52	Shaafi Aslam/ Swahili Dialect
Congo	30	3	French
Djibouti	5	NS*	French
Ethiopia	35-40	NS	Amharic
Equatorial Guinea	38	NS	Spanish
Gabon	22	5	French
The Gambia	29	12	English
Ghana	43	18	English
Guinea	14	4	French
Guinea Bissau	25	13	Portuguese
Ivory Coast	45	24	French
Kenya	60	35	English
Lesotho	58	82	English
Liberia	30	12	English

COUNTRY	% OF MALES	% OF FEMALES	OFFICIAL LANGUAGE
Madagascar	41	27	Malagasy
Malawi	48	25	English
Mali	13	1	French
Mauritania	17	NS	French
Mauritius	86	72	English
Mozambique	44	23	Portuguese
Namibia	45	31	English/Afrikaans
Niger	14	8	French
Nigeria	46	23	English
Rwanda	62	37	French
Sao Torret	5-10	NS	Portuguese
Principe	NS	NS	
Seengal	31	14	French
Sierra Leone	10	4	English
Seychelles	56	60	English/French
Somalia	60 (1978)	NS	Somali
South Africa	99 (whites) 50 (Africans)	NS	Afrikaans/English
Sudan	38	14	Arabic
Swaziland	57	53	English
Tanzania	78	70	English
Togo	27	7	French
Uganda	65	40	English
Upper Volta	18	5	French
Western Sahara	20	NS	Arabic
Zambia	79	58	English
Zaire	77	39	French
Zimbabwe	78	64	English

*NS = not supplied.

Source of Table I: Compiled from Jane Martin (ed.), *Global Studies: Africa*, Guilford, Conn.: The Dushkin Publishing Group, Inc., 1985; twenty years later, Africa's educational picture has not radically changed for the African masses, see Global Studies Africa (1997).

> Illiteracy…is not only a disqualification from better paid employment in offices or factories. It is not only a cultural deprivation, an exclusion from national life, and in some countries even from voting. …To be illiterate is to be helpless in a modern state run by a way of complex laws and regulations. The man who cannot read or write is at the mercy of those who can. He is totally dependent on the sometimes questionable honesty and competence of lawyers and officials. …He is a sitting duck for exploitation and fraud. Illiteracy, like other forms of educational disadvantages, weighs heaviest on the groups who are already disadvantaged in other ways. …Illiteracy is concentrated among lower-income groups, the marginal masses and women.[41]

The masses of people starving in Africa are the illiterates, the half-educated who have prematurely dropped out of school and remain perpetually unemployed and frustrated. The African illiterates and half-educated continue to suffer from malnutrition, inadequate housing and other 'primitive' standards of living. Until African leaders implement massive programs to eradicate illiteracy, the people will continue to be the least developed in the world and their natural resources will continue to develop other areas of the globe other than Africa itself.[42]

African educational systems have not integrated continental Africa, nor have they eliminated tribalism and colonial mentality within individual African countries. African schools have not been used to attack the most salient and massive problems of starvation, malnutrition, underdeveloped agriculture and political stagnation of the masses of African people. The mis-educated minority continue to exploit, misdirect and mismanage Africa's natural resources.

> The problems that African (schools) face are bigger than can be solved on an individual basis or on national platform alone. International cooperation, both on regional and continental levels is not only long overdue, but imperative. The necessity for a united effort was perceived as long ago as the early days of independence when it was hoped that higher education would 'ensure the unification of Africa' and that expensive facilities like medicine and veterinary science would be joint enterprises across national boundaries. But the prospect of concerted effort in…education remains today as remote as it did in 1961 when this wish was so ardently and hopefully expressed.[43]

In closing, it must be emphasized that the continued starvation in Africa is the result of Africa's backwardness in politics, technology, education, agricultural production and in leadership. All countries that have effective and productive leadership make room or have savings for natural disasters such as floods, avalanches, earthquakes, and others generally beyond human control. Responsible governments are not only concerned with immediate exigencies, but also have plans for the future and seek out ways and means of achieving these plans. Because Africa has not been economically prepared to deal with massive starvation, the peasant, illiterates, and their children are left to the mercy of international food aid from some compassionate

African, American, and European countries.

Chapter Four

International Food Aid and its Effects

"There is," according to Walter Lippmann, "a...triangular relationship between the scene of action, the human picture of that scene, and the human response to that picture working itself out upon the scene of action."[1] The scene of action is in Africa, and the picture is one of millions of Africans starving in Somalia, Sudan and more than twenty other African countries. The pictures of hungry Africans have been brought to Americans and the rest of the world via television, radio, newspapers, magazines and other media. The American government, public and various social and religious organizations have responded generously. But what is food aid? What are the effects of food aid, or any type of aid?

Various views have been expressed with respect to America and other countries aiding Third World countries. There are those who advocate lifeboat ethics;[2] others spaceship ethics;[3] yet still others who advocate humanitarianism, national interests, or political expediency. Lifeboat ethics does not favor the sharing of resources, and views starvation as essentially a national problem which must not be abated by those who are wealthy, premised on the notion that the lifeboat can contain only so many people. Those who advocate the spaceship concept view the world as a single cosmos that has interdependent constituents, one of which, when affected, affects the whole cosmos. The religious and the humanitarians see starvation in human terms, and can, to a certain extent, sympathize and empathize with human beings dying because of lack of food and water. Politicians mostly see food aid in terms of foreign policy, their national interests and political ideology.

Generally, however, most Americans support the humanitarian concerns of aid to Third World countries and to Africa in particular. The young and well-educated segment of white America support food aid to Africa; African Americans, despite their general low economic and educational positions, are strong supporters of food aid to Africa, because perhaps they, more than most Americans, know how it feels to be hungry!

American aid to foreign countries has had a long history, and has been used for several reasons. After World War II, the United States expended close to two percent of its GNP, the largest foreign aid so far, to reconstruct Europe and Japan. This was the Marshall Plan. "The intention of the Marshall Plan was to provide the United States with a first line of defense against possible Russian aggression."[4] At the time, the fear of the spread of communism to Western Europe was behind United States' interests in providing such a massive aid and to a certain extent that fear of communism was the reason for U.S. aid to certain African countries in the 1960s or Post Colonial Africa. Sudan, Ghana, Zaire, Somalia, Kenya and Egypt could be cited as examples.

In 1954, the United States government promulgated PL 480 to provide aid to poorer countries that were at the periphery of the communist countries. "PL 480 evolved from a surplus disposal program – a relief valve for U.S. policy to maintain farm incomes – to a program figuring prominently in efforts to achieve…international political economic aims in a world confronting food scarcities."[5]

Food aid was then a political weapon and was used to get rid of surplus grains that was costing the U.S. government money. "By the early 1960s, U.S. grain surpluses were running in excess of 230 million tons and were costing U.S. tax payers billions of dollars in payments for farmers and for storage costs each year."[6] Between 1965 and 1966, the United States contributed more than 10 billion tons of grain to India, and by 1969, India had gained self-sufficiency in grain production. By the 1970s, "food aid became an instrument, not primarily of aid for development, but U.S. foreign policy."[7] The decline in Soviet grain production in 1972 made food an international political commodity. As grain crops became scarce, producing countries such as the United States could use food as a political weapon and could select countries, based on ideological affinity, to which it chose to sell. As the oil-producing countries used their commodity for economic and political reasons, so did the United States use its food surplus. South Vietnam, Egypt and other countries received large tonnages of food aid; Sahelian drought-stricken countries also received food aid from the United States, but "The principal form of food aid has not been outright gifts, but rather concessional sales where recipient countries purchase commodities they need from the United States on long-term credit (up to 40 years) and at low interest rates because it would be difficult for them to pay commercial terms."[8] Once the terms have been met, the donor country might require that the food be transported in the donor country's ships, planes or vehicles. The transportation fees would be set high because the donor country knows that the recipient country has no other choice but to purchase the donor's facilities such as machinery. In the process, the shipping industry and other intermediaries such as the trucking industry make money. Unfortunately, however, "much of the U.S. public inappropriately persists in seeing food aid solely as an act of U.S. humanitarianism...foreign policy objectives are also served."[9] The two objectives, humanitarianism and foreign policy considerations, are not mutually exclusive.

While the United States government has contributed more than 300 million dollars worth of food aid to Africa,[10] there is also the concern for the poor within the United States itself and generally, "there is considerably more optimism about the feasibility of solving U.S. poverty problems compared to solving those of the developing countries."[11] Private organizations such as Africare, Care, American Red Cross, Oxfam and private individuals have, out of humanistic reasons, also contributed greatly, by helping the victims of the African famine, and one cannot help but be grateful to these groups and individuals. But what are the effects of these aid projects on Africa?

There is no question that famine has had, and will continue to have negative effects on the victims, including those who will survive. The famine has isolated Africa as weak and in the international arena, Africa and African people have low prestige. The children who will survive the famine will be greatly affected; their mental and physical capacities would be substantially hampered. Under these conditions, a generation of Africa's youth becomes a liability in terms of the contribution they could make to rapid economic development of the African continent.

The starvation in Africa has had negative effects on Africans in the diaspora; if in the 1960s they were proud and identified with Africa, in the 1980s, 1990s and so on, they have been ashamed of Africa; the constant pictures on television of dying Africans have created negative images and these affect African-Americans most directly. To a certain extent, Europeans could be quietly congratulating themselves in saying that blacks cannot really care of themselves, for within forty to fifty years of independence, Africans have still not been able to improve their economies, and have instead become international beggars of food. Furthermore, food aid, as humanitarian as it could be, has a taint of charity, and very few people can boast of, or be proud of being a charity case; it has psychological effects on both the donor and the recipient. In a sense, the recipient could be psychologically and politically asked to be fidel to the donor. A Kenyan researcher has opined that,

> There is a growing danger in Third World countries to think first of food aid when suggesting the means of fighting hunger. Yet, the consequences of food aid can be extremely devastating – economically, socially and politically. Economically, food aid generates dependency and thus erodes the people's initiative to produce sufficient food locally. This leaves room for exploitation by the agribusiness concerns interested in dominating the food market and reaping huge profits. It is also common knowledge that donor nations, especially the USA, see food aid as a means of disposing of surplus grain which cannot find a market and is therefore an embarrassment to them. In many cases food given as aid has been in store for too long and is not fit for human consumption, and even unfit for animal consumption in America...worse still, the food given is generally the wrong type, given in large quantities and carelessly administered, resulting in immediate serious physiological and medical problems.[12]

In certain cases, food aid could be substituted for agricultural reform, create dependency on the donor country, and licenses the latter country "...to exert political pressures on the governments of the developing countries and intervene in their internal affairs."[13] Food aid depresses food prices in the recipient country for local farmers, encourages inadequate agricultural policies[14] and changes the tastes of the local population in the recipient country which will continue to purchase the new foods or grains that might not be cultivable in the recipient country. In this way, African countries become dependent on the donor countries who have supplied new types of foodstuffs and results invariably in the emergence of alien dietary habits. The illiterate population lacks the appropriate knowledge to prepare new foodstuffs properly, and in cases such as powdered milk in the hands of illiterate African mothers, wrong measures of water and milk have been known to be given to young babies who later experience stomach problems.

Generally, food aid has had the reputation of being haphazardly distributed and coordinated. Though such aids are usually earmarked for the most needy in rural areas, urban poor have been known to reach food aid before those in rural areas. This has prolonged the starvation in rural areas. The urban poor often sell some of the food aid in the cities in order to buy local foodstuffs to which their taste buds have become used.

There is competition between Western governments involved in aiding Africa and private relief organizations such as World Vision, Church World Service, etc. The government concentrates on particular African countries such as Somalia, Sudan, and certain Sahelian countries, while private and religious organizations tend to be concerned not so much with politics, but with humanitarianism in general. The public tends to be suspicious of government attempts at aid because of its inefficiency and heavy reliance on political, ideological and foreign policy considerations. "...major religious agencies are popular with donors because of their reputation for efficiency and low administrative overhead."[15] However, major religious organizations have tended to mix humanitarian concerns with trying to 'convert' the victims of starvation into their own religious denominations. The Bible and food have often accompanied each other into relief camps, when the people's need is 'simply' food.[16] Some relief organizations have advertised themselves more, with respect to the work they are doing in Africa, than the effect or results of their work in the starving countries. Will they be able to continue to support the survivors of starvation in terms of providing healthy nutrition, education, housing, etc.?

Certainly, "food aid...(is) a short-term necessity in cases of famine..."[17] but does not solve the long-term problems of African nations. International aid is limited in the considerations of international relations, political ideology and affinity. Poverty in those countries that already over-produce must be solved. International trade and technological transfer problems have to be considered and dealt with. Furthermore, people seeking food aid have become too numerous to be satisfied adequately. Eastern Europe and other world regions are now also deserving of food aid; Western donors are also becoming overwhelmed with requests for all types of aid. African countries must themselves improve their societies in the area of food production. Africa must develop its food production as a starting point to increase "its negotiating strength…on the global chessboard"[18] of politics, economics and social development.

THE AGENCIES

ADVENTIST DEVELOPMENT AND RELIEF AGENCY
6840 Eastern Avenue, NW, Washington, DC 20012 (202) 722-6770

AFRICAN INLAND MISSION
135 West Crooked Hill Road, Pearl River, NY 10965

AFRICARE
1601 Connecticut Ave. NW, Washington, DC 20009 (202) 462-3614

AMERICAN FRIENDS SERVICE COMMITTEE
1501 Cherry Street, Philadelphia, PA 19102 (215) 241-7000

AMERICAN JEWISH JOINT DISTRIBUTION COMMITTEE
60 East 42nd Street, New York, NY 10165 (212) 687-6200

AMERICAN RED CROSS, "AFRICA RELIEF"
43 E. Ohio Street, Chicago, IL 60611 (312)440-2000

BAPTIST WORLD AID
1628 16th Street NW, Washington, DC 20009

CARE
660 First Ave., New York, NY 10016 (212) 686-3110

CATHOLIC RELIEF SERVICES
P.O. Box 2045, Church Street Station, New York, NY 10008 (212)
838-4700

CHRISTIAN CHILDREN'S FUND
P.O. Box 26511, Richmond, VA 23261

CHRISTIAN REFORMED WORLD MISSIONS
2850 Kalamazo Ave., SE, Grand Rapids, MI 49560

CHURCH WORLD SERVICE
475 Riverside Drive, New York, NY 10115 (212) 870-2257
DIRECT RELIEF INTERNATIONAL
P.O. Box 30820, Santa Barbara, CA 93130 (805) 687-3694

GRASSROOTS INTERNATIONAL
Box 312, Cambridge, MA 02139 (617) 497-9180

HEIFER PROJECT INTERNATIONAL
P.O. Box 808, Little Rock, AR 72203

INTERCHURCH MEDICAL ASSISTANCE
Box 429, New Windsor, MD 21776 (301) 635-6474

LUTHERAN WORLD RELIEF
360 Park Ave. South, New York, NY 10010 (212) 532-6350

MAP INTERNATIONAL
Box 50, Wheaton, IL 60187 (800) 225-8550

MENNONITE CENTRAL COMMITTEE
21 South 12 Street, Akron, PA 17501 (717) 859-1151

OXFAM
115 Broadway Boston, MA 02116 (617) 482-1211

PROJECT MERCY
7237 Leo Road, Fort Wayne, IN 46825 (219) 484-9477

SALVATION ARMY
1025 Vermont Ave. NW, Washington, DC 20005

SAVE THE CHILDREN
P.O. Box 925, Westport, CT 06881 (203) 226-7271

U.S. COMMITTEE FOR UNICEF
Box 3040, Grand Central Station, New York, NY 10163 (800) 826-1100

WORLD CONCERN DEVELOPMENT ORGANIZATION
19303 Freemont Ave., N., Seattle, WA 98133 (800) 426-7010

WORLD NEIGHBORS
5116 North Portland Ave., Oklahoma City, OK 73112

WORLD RELIEF CORPORATION
P.O. Box WRC, Wheaton, IL 60187 (800) 535-LIFE

WORLD VISION
919 W. Huntingdon Drive, Monrovia, CA 91016 (818) 357-7979

YWCA
135 West 50th Street, New York, NY 10020

The following groups can provide additional information about food and hunger issues:

BREAD FOR THE WORLD
Box 789, San Francisco, CA 94101 (415) 346-6100

THE HUNGER PROJECT
Box 789, San Francisco, CA 94101 (415) 346-6100

INSTITUTE FOR FOOD AND DEVELOPMENT POLICY
9588 Mission St., San Francisco, CA 94110 (415) 648-6090

RODALE PRESS
33 East Minor Street, Emmaus, PA 18049 (215) 967-5171

U.S. COMMITTEE FOR WORLD FOOD DAY
1001 22nd Street NW, Washington, DC 20437 (207) 653-2404

Chapter Five

Some Suggested Solutions to African Famine:

A Challenge to African and World Leaders

We have already dealt with Africa's natural as well as human resources, most of the countries afflicted by famine on the African continent, some of the factors associated with the famine and international food aid. We will now focus on some solutions to the ongoing famine and for the future so that such a large scale disaster could be abated.

Irrespective of the large scale food aid that has been received from Western, Eastern and African governments, African leaders retain the responsibility to develop Africa. They are the ones who publicly proclaim that they would rid Africa of corruption, colonialism, neo-colonialism and other forms of external and internal obstacles to mass development. They are expected to fulfill the promises they have made to the African masses that once the white man was gone, their lives would be greatly improved, or once the Emperor was gone and Marxism introduced, the local masses will be better off. They collect taxes from the masses, are in charge of exploiting Africa's natural resources such as gold, diamonds, bauxite, lumber, fish, petroleum and other natural and human resources. They are the educated ones from European, American and African universities and are known to make flamboyant speeches about the best and quickest means of raising the standards of living to the African populace. They have totally failed to deliver, as the evidence from the last forty to fifty years has shown. (See George B. N. Ayittey's Africa Betrayed (1992) and Africa in Chaos (1998).

It was in vogue in the sixties, and it is still popular today, to blame the Western imperialists for Africa's underdevelopment, "Africa is not in adequate control of its own resources. Indeed, the net beneficiaries of Africa's resources lie outside the African continent. Many of its mineral resources help to industrialize the rest of the world without necessarily improving the African condition itself."[1]

This has been known, at least for hundreds of years, but mere rhetoric about exploited Africa does not solve Africa's economic, social, cultural or political problems. African leaders must employ concerted, concrete mechanisms to alleviate Africa's poverty; starvation, bad housing and the general, continued deteriorating conditions of life. Famines, the worst case of underdevelopment,

> ...can be extremely costly to the nation. They result in human losses, emaciation, disease and malnutrition in infants. Experts argue that the production losses to the economy due to any famine amount to ten times the relief costs. (In Kenya) for

instance, records show that the relief costs during the 1961-62 famines were kshs. 100 million. This means that the production losses were kshs. 1,000 million – a fairly astronomical figure! Owing to these wide-ranging and prohibitive costs of hunger, clearly, the challenge of finding permanent solutions to (Africa's)...recurrent food shortages is a real one.[2]

A global strategy to slow down population growth and overconsumption in Western countries has also been suggested, for it has been found that "the symptoms of overconsumption and underconsumption are in many ways similar: impaired health and productivity, increased susceptibility to disease, and reduced life expectancy."[3] Obesity, a clear case of overconsumption, is well known in America and its concomitant ill effects. Other global strategies have been recommended which suggest Africans must be cognizant of their plight in resolving the problems facing them.

The Sahara desert, the largest in the world, and still expanding, must be 'reforested'. Massive efforts must be taken by African governments, near to the desert and farther from it, to plant trees in order to deter the progressive desert in claiming more land. "There must be a massive reforestation program throughout the drought stricken areas,...without such a plan, the ecology of the continent will be destroyed. The farmers are going to need machinery and seeds... We desperately need trees planted. The trees shade the earth from the sun and protect the earth against land erosion."[4] Reforestation of the massive Sahara undoubtedly requires a Pan-African input, and without reforestation, countries south of the Sahara – Mauritania, Mali, Niger, Chad, Senegal, etc. – will, in the next few years, begin to feel the presence of the Sahara and its consequences. Indeed, 'the ecology of the continent will be destroyed.' There is now sufficient warning to warrant commencement of reforestation. This feat would require Western, Eastern or Japanese technology, and it must be added that the developed countries must be concerned about desertification in Africa for they too would be affected with respect to global interdependence in the world market in terms of their need for raw materials and agricultural products.

African governments should create a Pan-African system of food reserves. Interestingly, for the African continent, "the concept of a food reserve is not new. Four thousand years ago Joseph of Egypt advised the Pharaohs that they should build reserves of grain during the fat years so as not to be caught short during the lean ones."[5] But as events have shown, "even this ancient and elementary wisdom seems to be beyond the reach of today's policy makers."[6]

African governments must turn away from prestige projects, mostly established in urban areas where they live, and concentrate on food production. There must be expansion in cultivable areas, especially in middle Africa, which is "…actually larger than the total agricultural area of the United States."[7] Here again, science and technology can be used to eradicate tsetse flies that cause sleeping sickness which in turn saps the energy of the human resource.

Water storage and irrigation methods are viable solutions for those African countries not blessed with adequate rainfall or large rivers. Extensive storage ponds can be dug to store water during the wet seasons to be used in the dry seasons on individual small or large farms. Using an old truck engine, water can be pumped from individual ponds onto the crops in the field. Such procedures are not highly scientific and African farmers must not depend on Westerners for simple methods of transferring water from where it is in abundance to where it is scarce. Irrigation is not a new science to African cultivators, for this has been extensively used in the Nile region.

In African secondary schools, colleges and universities, agricultural education should be an exigency and must be research oriented. The study of tropical agriculture with emphasis on seeds, length of growing seasons, type of soils in which particular crops can be most productively grown, to mention a few, are some of the areas that need particular attention. Settled agriculture, as opposed to nomadism or shifting cultivation, would in the long run prove to conserve African vegetation much more effectively. Improved agricultural practices such as the use of tractors on large scale farms will undoubtedly improve yields per acreage. The use of fertilizers has been recommended, but in certain cases, its overuse does damage to the soil; "...it is where fertilizers have been hitherto least used that they will do the most good."[8] Paradoxically, the countries that 'overproduce' spend much more on agricultural research, while those which 'underproduce' continue to be less concerned with agricultural research.

In science, Africa has lagged behind. "In 1965, the UNESCO conference on education held in Lagos, Nigeria, estimated that Africa will need 50,000 to 70,000 more scientists by 1980."[9] However, in 1970 there were "...only 200 scientists per million people in Africa as compared to 2,000 per million in Europe."[10] This has left Africa still dependent on Western scientists and researchers who go there as experts for a limited period of time. Africa has to train its own scientists and researchers to attack the exigent problems of malnutrition, tropical diseases, poor soil conditions and other problems associated with agricultural production and public health. Africa must radically increase its numbers of scientifically skilled personnel. Furthermore, African education must concentrate on educating Africans attuned to the "...economic realities"[11] of the continent and its people.

> The shortage of skilled labor is now found in the technical and managerial sectors of the economy. The surplus of educated persons without skills that directly relate to economic needs hinders development, for these persons often remain unemployed

and thus fail to contribute to the economy. By relying on the
traditional welfare system of the extended family for their
subsistence, they place an increased burden on that sector of the
gainfully employed population which already operates under a
high dependency ratio.[12]

Western experts have constantly exhorted African leaders to
concentrate on agricultural production, while they themselves, the
Western countries, advance industrially. While it is true that Africa
must improve its agricultural production, it must do so industrially.
It is only through industrial agriculture that Africa will be able to
produce in abundance, preserve, store, diversify and transport its
agricultural products from one sector of the continent to the other.
Poor transportation systems create Africa's liabilities for development,
slowing down the movement of people, goods and services. "Of the
continent's 57,000 miles of track, 13,800 miles are in South Africa."[13]
And "as for roads, only the Maghreb is adequate."[14] Because of
"under-industrialization,"[15]

> More than 75 percent of Africa's lumber leaves the continent
> as rough timber. And 98 percent of the phosphate undergoes no
> transformation before being sent to enrich the countries of the
> North – who are also major agricultural exporters and supply
> Africa with the food it cannot produce.[16]

Some Westerners have suggested technical assistance or
technological transfer from the developed countries into Africa,
but as of yet, it has not been effected, at least not in the scope of

the Marshall Plan for Western Europe. Though technical assistance should be encouraged, must Africans sit and wait for Europeans to hand out technology as they do food?

To a great extent, Africa's underdevelopment, of which the continued large scale starvation is a manifestation, is due to the failure of the concept of African unity or Pan-Africanism based on the Casablanca Charter.[17] The Lagos Charter that was signed in 1963 and which formed the OAU (Organization of African Unity) advocated cooperation, no interference in the internal affairs of other African states, etc. and was timorous about committing itself to complete unity as advocated by the radical Casablanca group, the minority group. However, the last forty to fifty years have shown that the minority can be right, while the majority could be wrong. We are now encouraged that the African Union will integrate Africa.

Some economists have recommended comparative advantage as a strategy for Third World development. This strategy would permit individual Third World countries to concentrate on producing goods they can produce cheaply, efficiently and effectively. But as African countries are not yet integrated, this developmental strategy would end up with African countries competing with each other in the world market since they produce the same sort of goods. Ivory Coast produces coffee, but so do Kenya, Liberia, Madagascar, Rwanda, Sao Tome and Principe; Angola produces cotton, but so do Benin, Cameroon, Central African Republic, Chad, Ivory Coast, Madagascar, Mali, etc. Various examples could be given that could further testify that African countries generally produce the same sort of agricultural products and sell them to the same customers in the West, where they compete with each other. Thus, without complete African Unity based on Nkrumah's position,[18] African countries will continue to compete with each other in the world market controlled by their ex-colonizers.

Economists have argued that continentally planned economic institutions would reduce duplication of industrial plants and create an integrated economy that would benefit the masses.

"...an integrated economy would have a central bank and a common currency. Such institutions would not only facilitate inter-state commerce and exchange but also mobilization and channeling of funds for development."[19]

Pan-African politicians and educators[20] have also argued for an integrated Africa. They view that Africa must be politically and institutionally integrated in order to have a strong and viable continent. The virtues of a United Africa are too numerous to list, but it can be noticed that under Pan-Africanism, starvation in Africa would not be seen or treated as an individual national problem, but as a Pan-African problem, and dealt with as such. Under Pan-Africanism, continental resources, such as the hydroelectric power resources in Central Africa, would be 'transferred' to the areas that are not so endowed. Under Pan-Africanists, Somalians, Chadians or Ethiopians in Sudan would not be viewed as refugees or aliens, because really, why should any African be seen as a foreigner in Africa? Is a New Yorker a foreigner in Mississippi? He is an out-of-stater, but not a foreigner! The challenge to Africa's economic and social backwardness such as starvation, malnutrition, bad housing, illiteracy and the rest is to improve agricultural production and feed the people first and foremost; above all, Africa must completely unite; for in unity there is strength and in strength there is power to deal with Pan-African problems such as starvation. Until Africa unites politically and economically, particular African countries will continue to experience starvation, malnutrition, etc. for many more years to come. Some African countries are too poor, naturally, to feed their growing populations. The answers to much of Africa's economic, social, cultural, political and refugee problems can be more effectively solved through a concerted effort. As Ayandele (1984) has observed, the problems that (Africans) face are bigger than can be solved on an individual basis or on the national. Cooperation both on regional and continental levels is not only long overdue, but imperative.[21] And in that imperative, lies the challenge to the present and future African and world leaders.

NOTES

CHAPTER ONE

AFRICA'S NATURAL RESOURCES

1. The 1985 Africa Diary, N.Y., New York: The Africa Letter, 1985, (See "Africa in Brief" section).

2. Ibid.

3. Ibid.

4. Ibid.

5. Ibid.

6. Andrew M. Kamarck, "The Resources of Tropical Africa," Daedalus: Journal of the American Academy of Arts and Sciences, Vol. III, No. 2 (Spring, 1982), p. 149.

7. Ibid., p. 151.

8. Ibid., p. 156.

9. Ibid.

10. Ibid., p. 157.

11. Ibid.

12. Ibid., p. 158.

NOTES

CHAPTER TWO

THE AFFLICTED COUNTRIES

1. Africa News, "The Hungry and the Hungriest: A Survey." <u>Africa News</u>, (Feb. 25, 1985), p. 16.

2. Ibid.

3. Ibid., p. 13.

4. Ibid., p. 11.

5. Ibid.

6. Ibid., p. 19.

7. Ibid.

8. Ibid., p. 12.

9. Ibid.

10. Ibid., p. 18.

11. Ibid.

12. W. W. McPherson (ed.), <u>Economic Development in Tropical Agriculture: Theory, Policy, Strategy, and Administration,</u> Gainesville, Florida: University of Florida Press, 1968, p. 5.

NOTES

CHAPTER THREE

WHY STARVATION IN AFRICA

1.   Jim Josling, "The World Food Problem: National and International Aspects," in Ross B. Talbot (ed.). The World Food Problem and U.S. Food Politics and Policies: 1972-1976. Ames, Iowa: Iowa State University Press, 1976, p. 1.

2.

3.   Sterling Wortman and Ralph W. Cummings, Jr., To Feed This World: The Challenge and the Strategy, Baltimore, Maryland: The Johns Hopkins University Press, 1978, p. 1.

4.   Colin Clark, Starvation or Plenty? N.Y., New York: Taplinger Publishing Company, 1970, see the foreword.

5.   Ibid., p. 35.

6.   Ibid., pp. 45-46.

7.   The Africa Letter, The 1985 Africa Diary, N.Y., New York: The Africa Letter, 1985; see the section – Africa in Brief.

8.   Joseph D. Tydings, Born to Starve, N.Y., New York: William Morrow and Company,

        Inc., 1970, p. 69.

9.   P. Markov, "The World Food Problem," in Ross B. Talbot (ed.), The World Food Problem and U.S. Food Politics and Policies, 1972-76. Ames, Iowa: Iowa State University Press, 1977, p. 17.

10.   Tydings, op. cit., p. 80.

11. Ibid., p. 55.

12. Ibid., p. 56.

13. Ibid., p. 57.

14. Tibor Mende, <u>From Aid to Re-Colonization: Lessons of a Failure</u>, N.Y., New York: Pantheon Books, 1973, p. 60.

15. Marilyn Silberfein, "The African Cultivator: A Geographical Overview," in Alan K. Smith and Claude E. Welch, Jr. (eds.), <u>Peasants in Africa</u>, Brandeis University, Waltham, Mass: African Studies Association, 1978, p. 7.

16. Charles Ebel, "Africa's Failing Agriculture: Battling the Odds," Africa News (February 5, 1985), p. 4.

17. Ibid.

18. Ibid.

19. Ibid., p. 5.

20. Ibid.

21. Ibid.

22. Ibid.

23. Ras Makonnen, <u>Pan-Africanism From Within</u>, Oxford University Press, 1973, p. 241.

24. <u>Africa Now</u> (March, 1982) , p. 18.

25. Radiala Onim, "Oloitiptip's Fall From Grace to Grass," <u>New African</u> (March, 1985), p. 31.

26. Edmond J. Keller, "Decolonization and the Struggle for Independence," in Phyllis M. Martin and Patrick O'Meara (eds.),

Africa, Bloomington, Indiana: Indiana University Press, 1977, p. 163.

27.   Bernard Lewis, Race and Color in Islam, Harper & Row Publishers, 1971, pp. 65-66.

28.   Walter Rodney, A History of the Upper Guinea Coast 1545-1800, New York: Monthly Review Press, 1980.

29.   Ibid., p. 196.

30.   Ibid., p. 195.

31.   Ibid., p. 253.

32.   Onim, op. cit.

33.   Walter Rodney, How Europe Underdeveloped Africa, Washington, D.C.: Howard University Press, 1974.

34.   Abdul Rahman Mohamed Babu, African Socialism or Socialist Africa? Dar es Salaam, Tanzania Publishing House, 1981 , p. 35.

35.   Ibid., p. 43.

36.   See Jema Martin (ed.) Global Studies: Africa, Guilford, Conn.: The Dushkin Publishing Group, Inc. 1985.

37.   Okot P'Bitek, Africa's Cultural Revolution, Nairobi, MacMillan Books for Africa, 1973, p. 102.

38.   Emmanuel A. Ayandele, "Africa: The Challenge of Higher Education," Daedalus: Journal of the American Academy of Arts and Sciences (Spring, 1982), p. 168.

39.   Ibid.

40.   Ibid.

41.   See the whole issue of Africa Now (March, 1982).

42. Paul Harrison, <u>Inside the Third World, the Anatomy of Poverty</u>, Penguin Books, 1982, p. 305.

43. Ali A. Magrui, <u>The African Condition: A Political Diagnosis</u>, Cambridge University Press, 1980, p. 114.

44. Ayandele, op. cit., p. 176.

NOTES

CHAPTER FOUR

INTERNATIONAL FOOD AID AND ITS EFFECTS

1.   T. Ross B. Talbot (ed.), <u>The World Food Problem and U.S. Food</u> <u>Politics and Policies: 1972-1976</u>, Ames, Iowa: Iowa State University Press, 1977, p. 25.

2.   Garrett Hardin, "A 'Doomsday' Perspective," in Talbot, op. cit., pp. 63-70.

3.   Ibid., p. 64.

4.   David Wall, <u>The Charity of Nations: The Political Economy of</u> <u>Foreign Aid</u>, New York: Basic Books, Inc., 1973, p. 9.

5.   Martin Kriesberg, "Food Aid and Foreign Policy (Part 2)," in Talbot, op. cit.,

        p. 244.

6.   Ibid. p. 242.

7.   Ibid. p. 243.

8.   Ibid. p. 244.

9.   Ibid. p. 247.

10.   <u>Ebony</u> (March, 1985), p. 45.

11.   Paul A. Laudicina, "World Poverty and Development: A Survey of American

        Opinion," in Talbot, op. cit., p. 74.

12.   C. Odegi-Awuondo, "Food Crisis Could Be Most Explosive," <u>The</u> <u>Weekly Review</u>,

(February 10, 1984), p. 19.

13.   P. Markov, "The World Food Problem," in Talbot, op. cit., p. 19.

14.   Paul J. Isenman and H.W. Singer, "Food Aid: Disincentive Effects and Their

Policy Implications," in Talbot, op. cit., pp. 248-249.

15.   Charles Ebel, "Africa's Failing Agriculture: Battling the Odds," Africa News

(Feb. 25, 1985), p. 7.

16.   Ibid.

17.   Ibid., p. 5.

18.   Sophie Bessis, "The Fruits of Independence: Burgeoning Urbanization, Lagging

Industrialization," in Jane Martin (ed.), Global Studies: Africa, Guilford, Conn., The Dushkin Publishing Group, Inc., 1985, pp. 12-14.

NOTES

CHAPTER FIVE

SOME SUGGESTED SOLUTIONS TO THE AFRICAN FAMINE:

A CHALLENGE TO AFRICAN AND WORLD LEADERS

1.   Ali A. Mazrui, The African Condition, Cambridge University Press, 1980, p. 114.

2.   C. Odegi-Awuondo, "Food Crisis Could Be Explosive, The Weekly Review, (Feb. 10, 1984), p. 19.

3.   Garrett Hardin, "A 'Doomsday' Perspective," in Ross B. Talbot (ed.), The World Food Problem and U.S. Food Politics and Policies: 1972-1876, Ames, Iowa: Iowa State University Press, 1977., p. 66; Hardin's article was published in Psychology Today (September, 1974) as "Lifeboat Ethics – The Case Against Helping the Poor."

4.   Lester R. Brown, "The Politics and Responsibility of the North American Breadbasket," in Ross B. Talbot, op. cit., p. 50.

5.   Ebony, March, 1985, p. 46, 48.

6.   Lester R. Brown, op. cit., p. 52.

7.   Brown, op. cit., p. 52.

8.   D. Gale Johnson, "World Food Problems and Prospects," in Talbot, op. cit., p. 265.

9.   Colin Clark, Starvation or Plenty? New York: Taplinger Publishing Company, 1970, p. 92.

10.   Joseph D. Tydings, Born to Starve, New York: William Morrow and Company, Inc. 1970, p. 58.; see also Pauline Hountondji's and

Judi W. Wakhungu's (2002), "Scientific Dependence in Africa" and "The Baby on the Back; Science, Technology, and Politics of Progress in Africa." In Asumah, Johnston-Anumonwo, and Marah, editors, The Africana Human Condition and Global Dimensions. Binghamton, NY, Binghamton University, Global Publications, pp. 83-116.

11. Tydings , p. 59.

12. Ibid.

13. Ibid., p. 60.

14. Sophie Bessis, "The Fruits of Independence: Burgeoning Urbanization, Lagging Industrialization," in Jane Martin (ed.), Global Studies: Africa, Guilford, Conn., The Dushkin Publishing Group, Inc., 1985, p. 17.

15. Ibid.

16. Ibid.

17. Kwame Nkrumah, Revolutionary Path, N.Y., International Publishers, 1973, pp. 233-248.

Dr. Nkrumah's brand of Pan-Africanism suggested a continental economic and industrial plan, an African common market, an African currency and monetary zone, a central bank, common foreign policy and defense, a continental communications system and a common African citizenship!

18. Africa Must Unite, New York: International Publishers, 1970.

19. Ann Seidman and Reginald H. Green, Unity or Poverty: The Economics of Pan-Africanism, Baltimore, Maryland: Penguin

Books, 1968. See also Tetteh A. Kofi, "The Need for the Principles of a Pan-African Economic Ideology." <u>Civilizations</u> XXVI, 3-4: 205-231; N.A. Cox-George, "The Political Economy of African Unity," <u>Presence Africaine</u>, No. 31, Vol. 3 (1960), pp. 9-24; Shibabaw Yimenu, "Pan-Africanism and African Economic Development," <u>The Black Scholar</u> (May, 1975), pp. 32-40.

20.   Haile Selassie, "Towards African Unity," <u>The Journal of Modern African Studies</u>, Vol. 1, No. 3 (1963), pp. 281-288; Nnamdi Azikwe, <u>Renascent Africa</u>, London: Frank Cass and Co., Ltd., 1968.

21.   Emmanuel A. Ayandele, "Africa: The Challenge of Higher Education," <u>Daedalus: Journal of the American Academy of Arts and Sciences</u> (Spring, 1982), p. 176.

ABOUT THE AUTHOR:

Dr. John Karefah Marah is a native of the Republic of Sierra Leone, West Africa, where he received his elementary and secondary education; he later attended Southwick High in Southwick, Massachusetts, the State University College of New York at Oneonta, Tuskegee Institute, Tuskegee, Alabama, and Syracuse University, Syracuse, NY. Dr. Marah is currently professor of African and Afro-American Studies at the State University of New York College at Brockport where he teaches African -American Literature, The Black Woman Today, African Politics, and Exploring the Black Experience. Dr. Marah has appeared on television as well as radio in Rochester, NY, concerning starvation in Africa and Apartheid in South Africa; Dr. Marah has published extensively on Pan-Africanism and Education, including Pan-African Education: The Last Stage Of Educational Developments in Africa, (1989) and African People in the Global Village (1998).